The Scale Of... NATURAL LANDMARKS

By Joanna Brundle

BookLife PUBLISHING

©2019
BookLife Publishing Ltd.
King's Lynn
Norfolk PE30 4LS

All rights reserved.
Printed in Malaysia.

A catalogue record for this book is available from the British Library.

ISBN: 978-1-78637-882-8

Written by:
Joanna Brundle

Edited by:
Emilie Dufresne

Designed by:
Jasmine Pointer

All facts, statistics, web addresses and URLs in this book were verified as valid and accurate at time of writing. No responsibility for any changes to external websites or references can be accepted by either the author or publisher.

Photocredits

All images courtesy of Shutterstock.com. With thanks to Getty Images, Thinkstock Photo and iStockphoto.

Front Cover – Bluehousestudio, robuart, Moloko88, Ilyafs, runLenarun. 2–3 Amanita Silvicora. 4–5 – asantosg. 6–7 – Tomacco. 8–9 – ginger1, Anastasia Boiko. 10–11 – labzazuza. 12–13 – Fancy Tapis, JBOY, VectorShow, Panda Vector. 14–15 – LineTale, FMStox. 16–17 – SaveJungle, Sentavio. 18–19 – MicroOne, Dark ink. 20–21 – Chalintra.B, Katrevich Valeriy. 22–23 – Ksenica Artbox.

CONTENTS

Page 4   Introduction
Page 6   Niagara Falls
Page 8   The White Cliffs of Dover
Page 10   Hyperion
Page 12   Uluru
Page 14   Table Mountain
Page 16   The Grand Canyon
Page 18   Mauna Kea
Page 20   Mount Everest
Page 22   The Great Barrier Reef and the Yangtze River
Page 24   Glossary and Index

Words that look like this can be found in the glossary on page 24.

INTRODUCTION

Height

Length

The scale of things means how one thing compares in size to another. In this book, we will be travelling around the world, comparing famous natural landmarks by looking at their height or length.

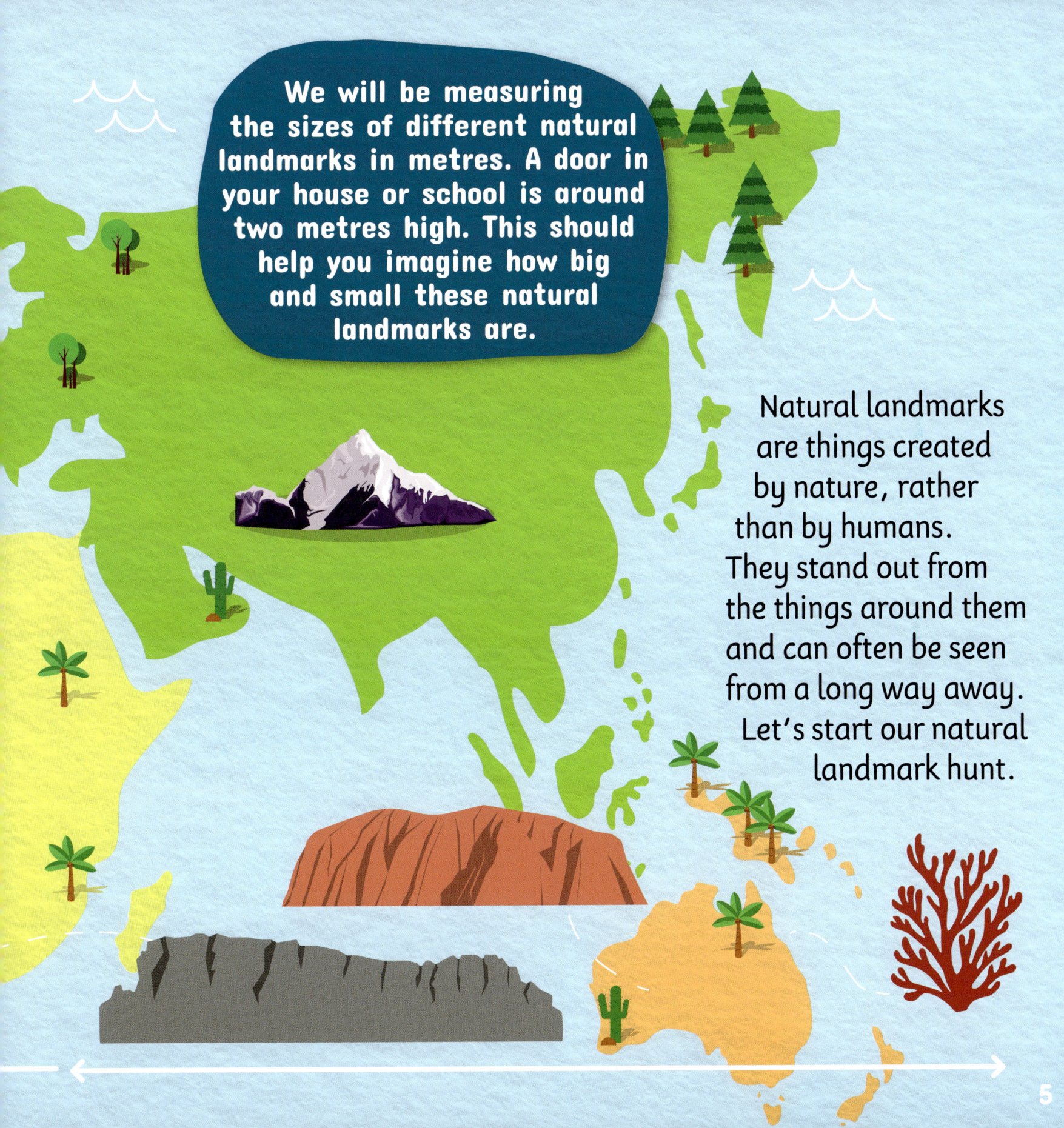

We will be measuring the sizes of different natural landmarks in metres. A door in your house or school is around two metres high. This should help you imagine how big and small these natural landmarks are.

Natural landmarks are things created by nature, rather than by humans. They stand out from the things around them and can often be seen from a long way away. Let's start our natural landmark hunt.

NIAGARA FALLS

Niagara Falls is the name given to three waterfalls that are on the border between Canada and the US. The Horseshoe Falls are the highest of the three. They are around 51 metres high.

51 metres

Niagara Falls

Canada

US

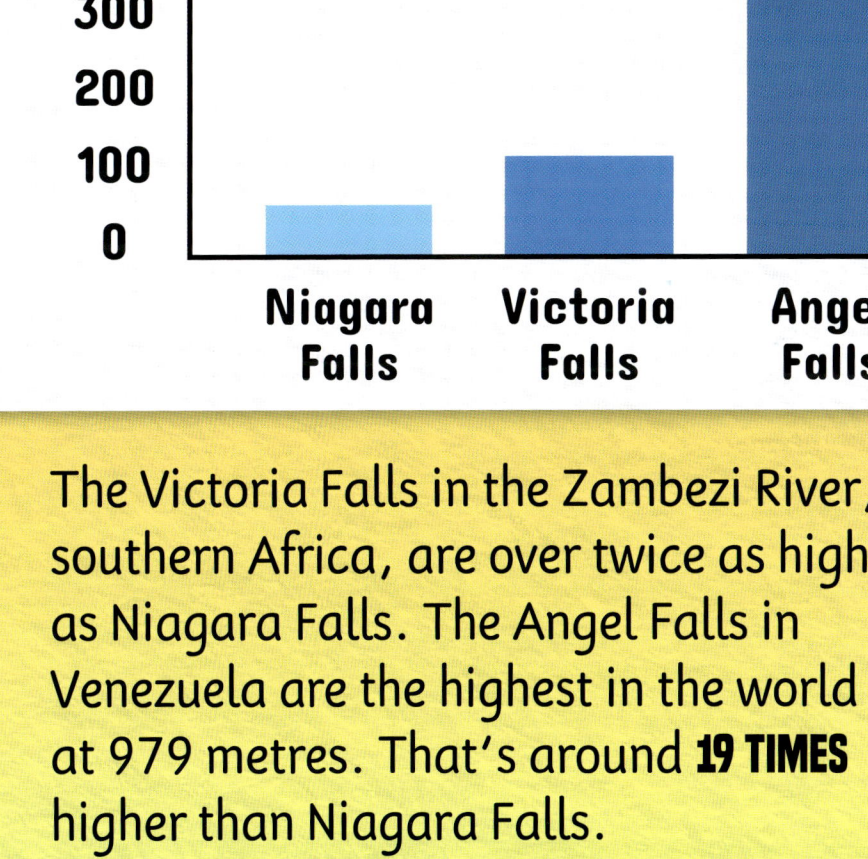

The Horseshoe Falls are about as high as 12 double decker buses piled on top of one another.

The Victoria Falls in the Zambezi River, southern Africa, are over twice as high as Niagara Falls. The Angel Falls in Venezuela are the highest in the world at 979 metres. That's around **19 TIMES** higher than Niagara Falls.

7

THE WHITE CLIFFS OF DOVER

The White Cliffs of Dover are part of the <u>coastline</u> of England. The cliffs are white because they are made of <u>chalk</u>. In places, they are over 100 metres high. That's around twice as high as Niagara Falls.

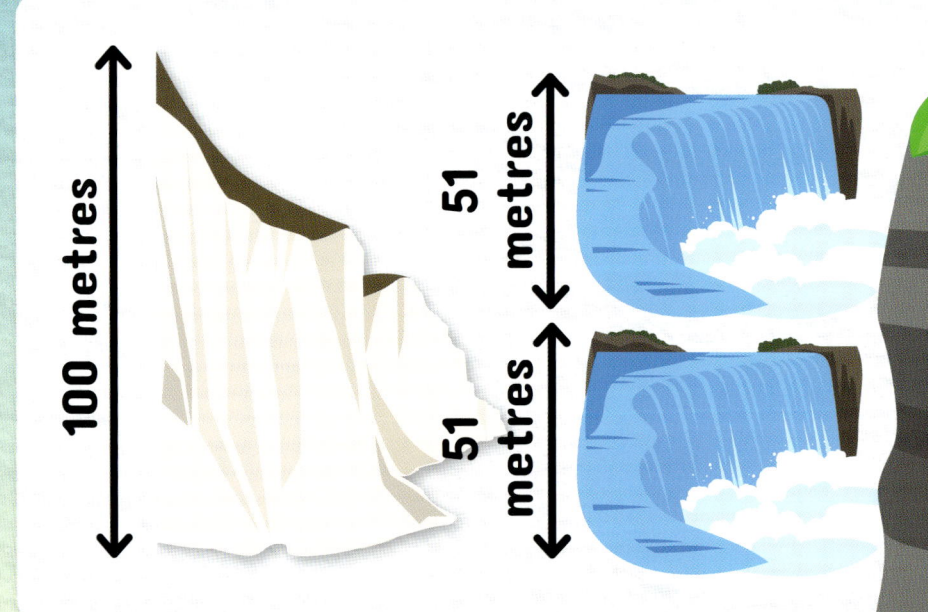

The White Cliffs of Dover

The Cliffs of Moher are in Ireland. They are 214 metres from the ground to their highest point. That's over twice as high as the White Cliffs of Dover.

The Cliffs of Moher

214 metres

The Cliffs of Moher were formed over 300 million years ago.

Hyperion

Hyperion is taller than 26 double decker buses stacked on top of one another.

Hyperion is the name given to a giant redwood tree. It is in a forest of redwood trees in California in the US. Hyperion is almost 116 metres tall.

116 metres

Scientists think that Hyperion is at least 600 years old. It is believed to be the tallest living thing on Earth.

California

Hyperion is taller than 68 adult humans standing on top of one another.

ULURU

Uluru is a giant rock in the middle of Australia. It is made of sandstone, and it rises 348 metres above the land around it. That is **THREE TIMES** as high as Hyperion.

Australia

Uluru

116 metres
116 metres
116 metres

348 metres

Dune 7 is a sand dune in the Namib desert in Namibia, Africa. It is 383 metres high. That makes Dune 7 as tall as Uluru with eight double-decker buses stacked on top.

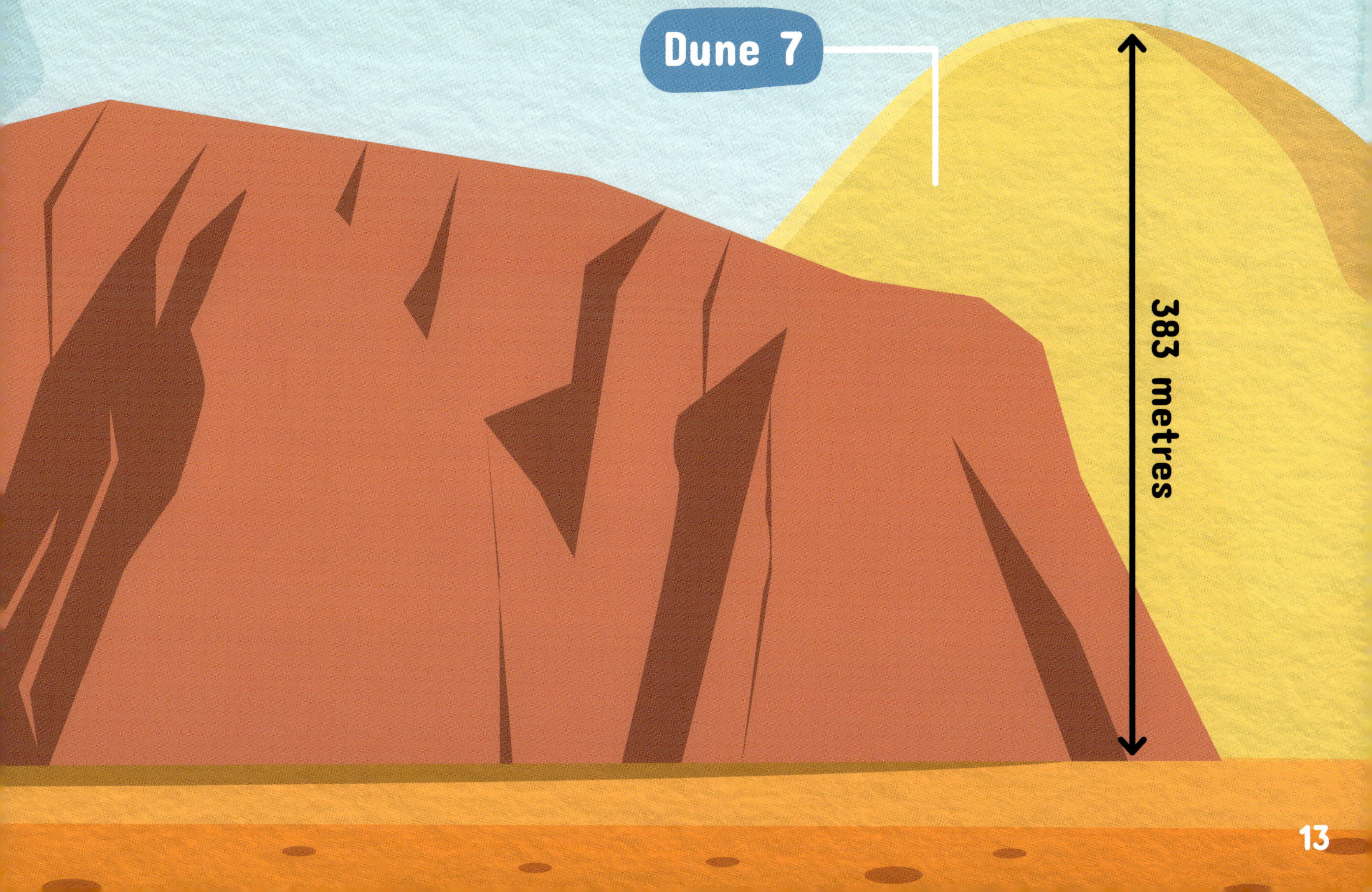

Dune 7

383 metres

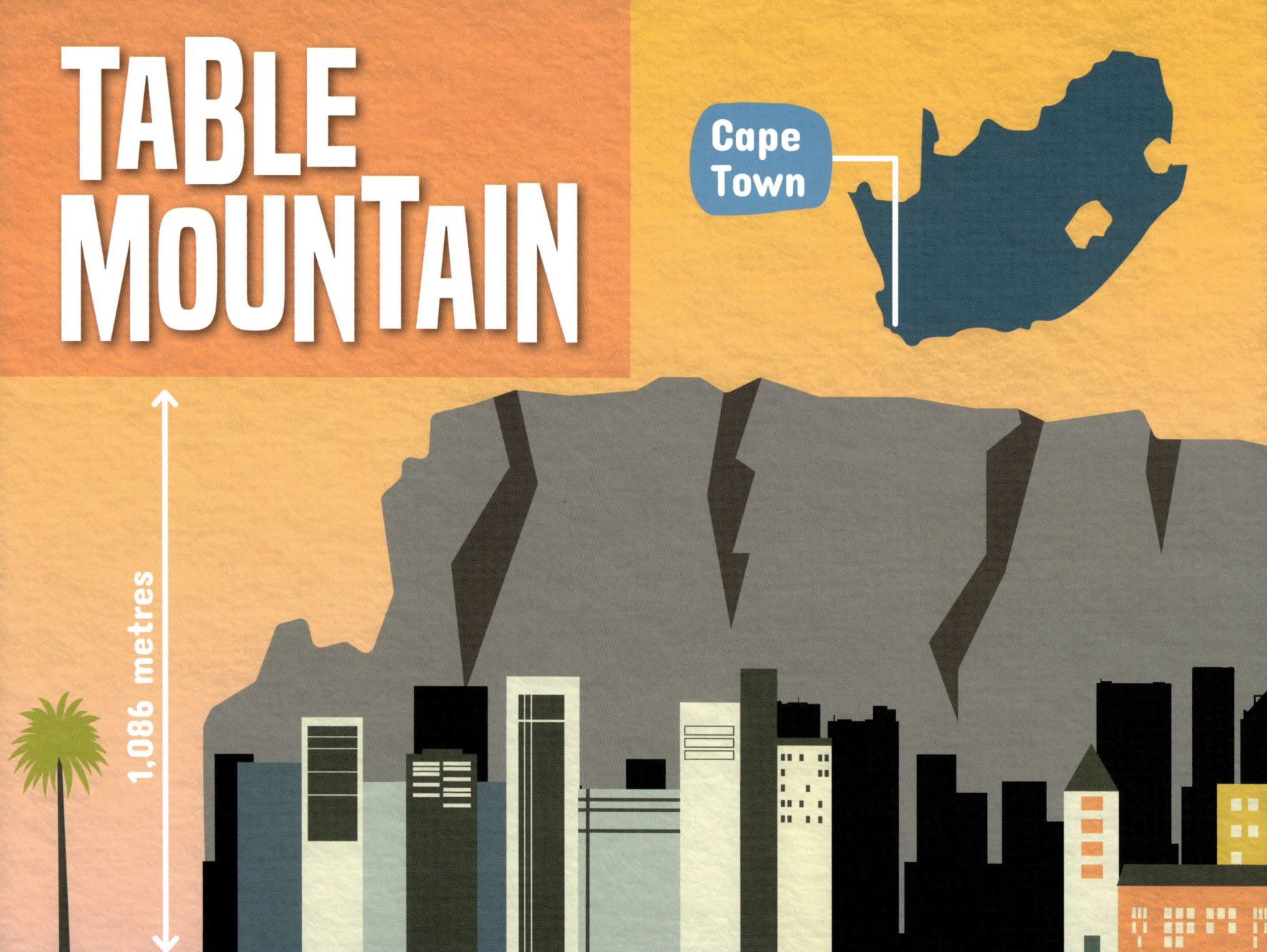

TABLE MOUNTAIN

Cape Town

1,086 metres

Table Mountain is a flat-topped mountain that looks like a table top. It looks over the city of Cape Town in South Africa. The mountain rises to 1,086 metres at its highest point.

Table Mountain is thought to be one of the oldest mountains in the world. Its rocks are about 600 million years old.

Table Mountain is more than **THREE TIMES** higher than Uluru.

THE GRAND CANYON

Grand Canyon

1,828 metres

Colorado River

The Grand Canyon is in Arizona in the US. Its steep sides were carved out by the Colorado River over millions of years. The Grand Canyon is 1,828 metres deep at its deepest point.

The Grand Canyon is 446 kilometres long. The total length of the Colorado River is 2,334 kilometres. This means that it is more than **FIVE TIMES** longer than the Grand Canyon.

**Colorado River
2,334 kilometres long**

**Grand Canyon
446 kilometres long**

A canyon is a deep, V-shaped valley, cut through rock by a river.

17

Mauna Kea

Mauna Kea is a volcano on the largest island of Hawaii. It hasn't erupted for thousands of years, but it could erupt again. Mauna Kea is 4,205 metres high.

On land, we can only see part of Mauna Kea. This part is more than twice as tall as the Grand Canyon is deep.

A large amount of Mauna Kea is under the sea. From the bottom of Mauna Kea under the sea to its top on land, it is actually around 10,000 metres tall.

Including the part under the sea, Mauna Kea is over **FIVE TIMES** higher than the Grand Canyon is deep.

MOUNT EVEREST

Mount Everest is 8,848 metres high and is the highest mountain in the world above the level of the sea. It is in Asia and is part of a group of mountains called the Himalayas.

Mount Everest is almost as high as five Grand Canyons piled up on top of one another.

Mount Everest

8,848 metres

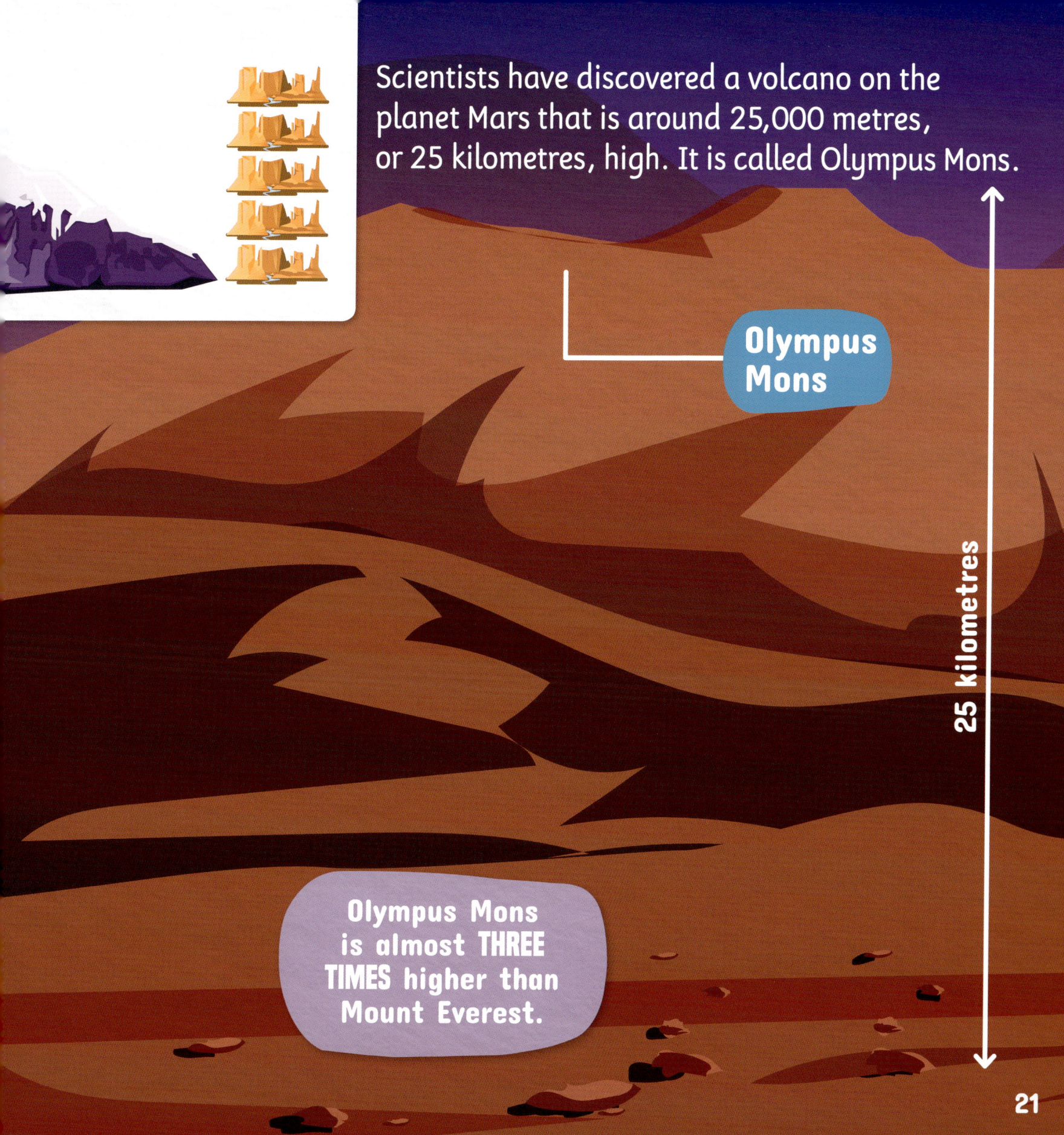

Scientists have discovered a volcano on the planet Mars that is around 25,000 metres, or 25 kilometres, high. It is called Olympus Mons.

Olympus Mons

25 kilometres

Olympus Mons is almost THREE TIMES higher than Mount Everest.

THE GREAT BARRIER REEF AND THE YANGTZE RIVER

Great Barrier Reef 2,300 kilometres

The Great Barrier Reef is the world's longest <u>coral reef system</u>. It is over 2,300 kilometres long and can be seen from space.

Coral is a simple sea animal that stays in one place and lives in groups. Corals make a hard, outside skeleton that helps build the reef.

22

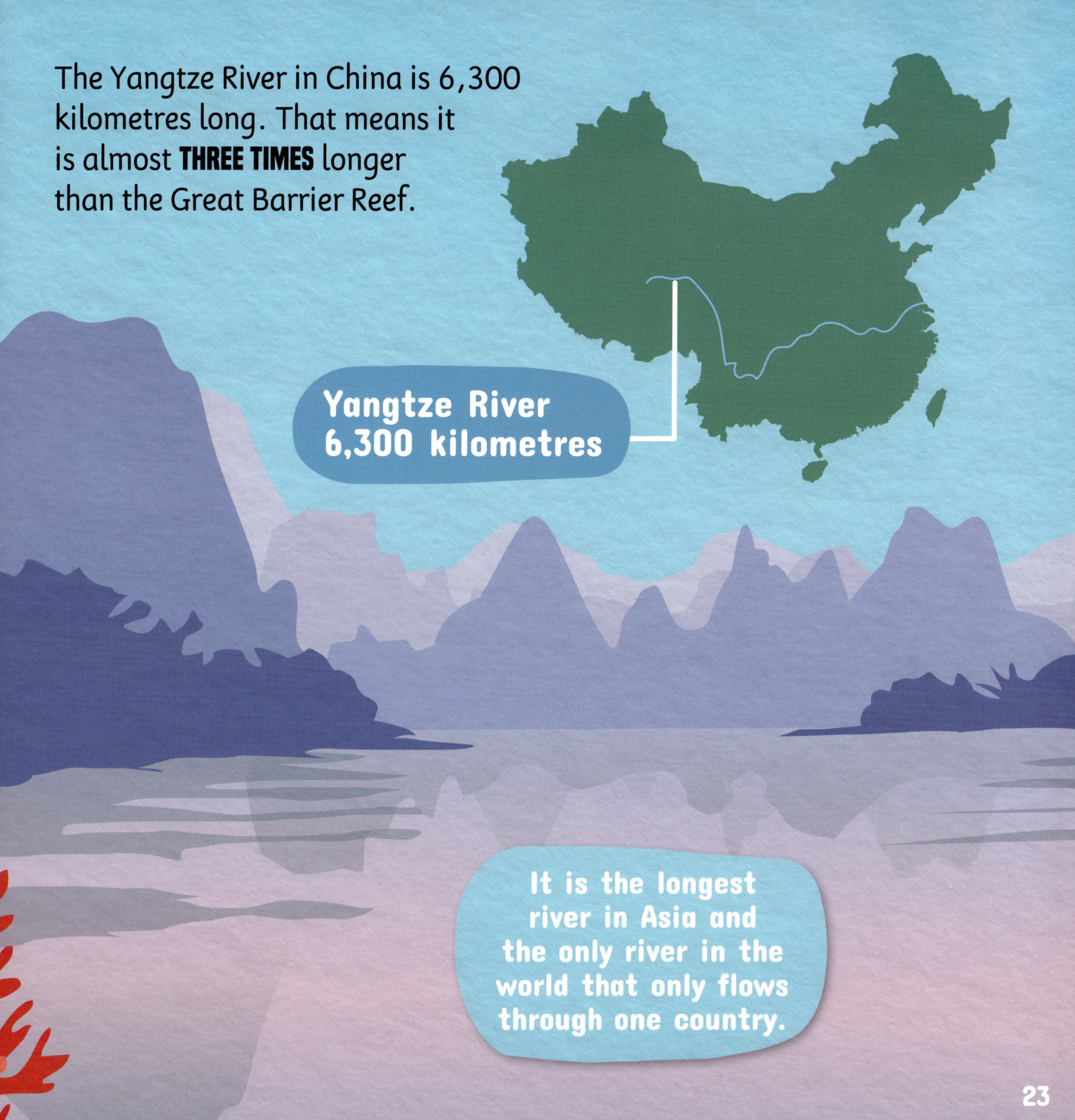

GLOSSARY

chalk	a soft, white rock that formed millions of years ago
coastline	the area along a coast where the land meets the sea
coral reef system	a long, narrow mass of corals and other things, usually found in warm seas
desert	a place that gets very little rain and where very few plants and animals can survive
erupted	sent out very hot, melted rock and gases in a sudden explosion
giant redwood	a very tall evergreen tree that produces cones and has brownish-red wood
sand dune	a hill or ridge of sand, formed into a variety of shapes by the wind
sandstone	a type of rock formed from grains of sand packed tightly together
volcano	a mountain that sometimes erupts, giving off very hot, melted rock and gases

INDEX

canyons 16–20
cliffs 8–9
coastlines 8
deserts 13
forests 10
mountains 14–15, 20–21
planets 21
rivers 7, 16–17, 23
rocks 12, 15, 17
sand dunes 13
seas 19–20, 22
trees 10
volcanoes 18, 21
waterfalls 6